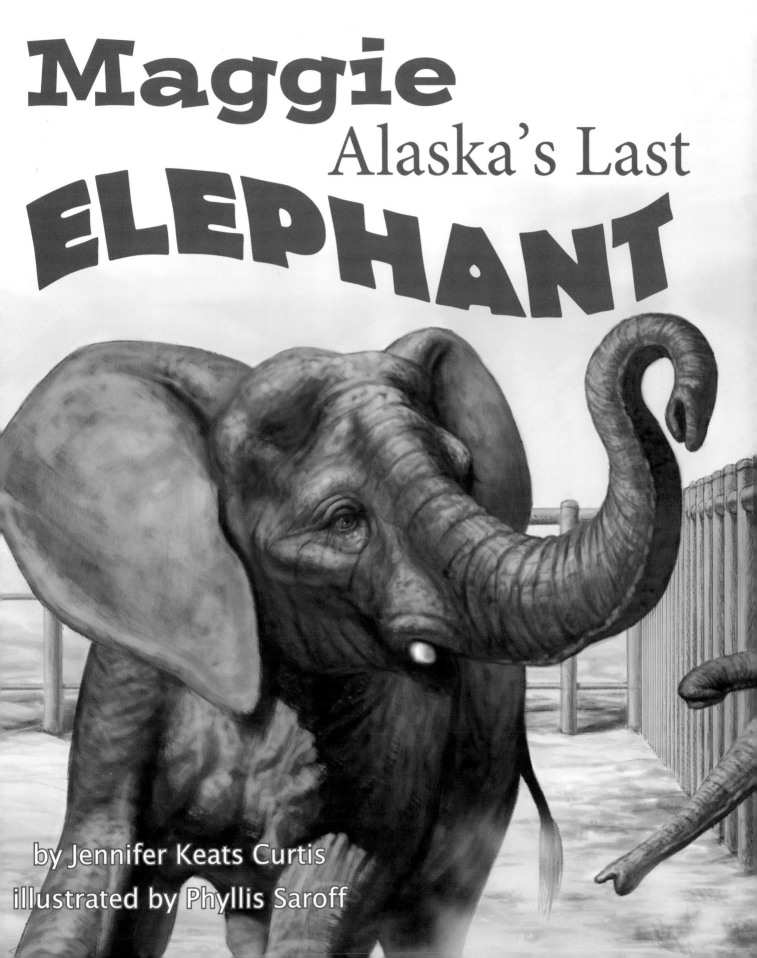

Maggie

Alaska's Last

ELEPHANT

by Jennifer Keats Curtis

illustrated by Phyllis Saroff

Once, elephants lived in Alaska—two of them. Annabelle, an Asian elephant, came first. She lived at the Alaska Zoo. Since elephants are herd animals and need friends, the keepers brought in baby Maggie, an African elephant, to keep Annabelle company.

Although the two were different species, the pair became friends. For years, despite the cold, the elephants were okay because they had each other. Then, Annabelle died.

Without Annabelle, Maggie seemed lost. Her keepers tried to cheer her up. When it snowed, they put mukluks (slippers) on her feet. When Maggie's feet got sore, her keepers cleaned them and filed her nails. On her birthday, her keeper Michelle painted her nails while checking her feet.

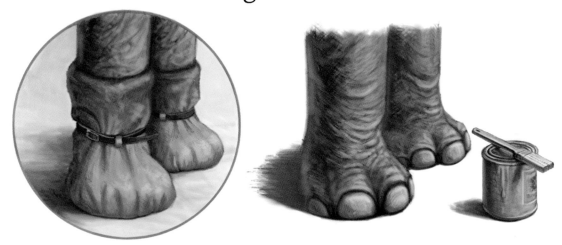

To get attention, Maggie honked loudly. The keepers encouraged the noise, the way we urge our dogs to bark when we say, "speak!" When Maggie got her shots from the vet, Michelle offered her candy. Maggie gently picked up this special treat with her two-fingered trunk.

Without another elephant, Maggie befriended a tire. She carried her tire everywhere. She flung it in the air with her trunk and caught it between her backside and a wall. At dinner time, Maggie propped up the tire. When she finished eating, she picked up the tire again. At night, when the keepers went home, Maggie curled the tire in her trunk. Each morning, the keepers returned to find lonely Maggie and her tire, waiting.

In the wild, elephants stay together as a loving family. Forever touching, they entwine their trunks, gently put their heads together, and lean on each other. When one elephant rests, another stands over her. Babies place their trunks into their mothers' mouths. They use their trunks to hold onto mommas' tails.

But, Maggie had no other elephant. She only had the tire.

Maggie's human friends worried about her. They built her a giant treadmill, which cost $150,000, so that she could exercise. Maggie didn't like the sound the treadmill made.

Alaskans loved having Maggie at their zoo, but fretted that a cold zoo was not the best place for one elephant.

One day, Maggie got sick. She lay down and couldn't get back up. Firefighters came to her rescue. They tried hoisting her up with a crane. Maggie was so heavy that the crane's motor broke. Finally, a second truck with a bigger motor heaved Maggie to her feet.

The staff knew it was time for Maggie to go. She needed a warm place with her own kind.

Fortunately, the Performing Animal Welfare Society (PAWS) in California wanted Maggie. PAWS rescues animals in need and is home to bears, lions, and two groups of elephants. And Maggie's keeper Michelle had just moved there.

The fastest way to move an 8,000-pound animal thousands of miles is on an enormous plane. The U.S. Air Force offered their cargo aircraft if someone would pay for the flight. A famous TV star heard about Maggie and wanted to help. He paid for her travel.

A giant crate was designed for Maggie. The inside was snug, with just enough room for Maggie to stand. It would be dangerous for her to lie down. She might not be able to get back up.

For weeks, trainers worked with Maggie. At first she was nervous and shuffled her feet as she walked into the crate. She would have to remain still for the long flight. It must have been scary, but smart, brave Maggie learned quickly. Each time she walked into the crate, she was a little calmer and stayed a little longer.

When it was time for Maggie to leave Alaska, she quietly walked into the crate, just as she'd been taught. A huge crane placed her crate on the back of a truck. As the truck drove through the zoo gates, Maggie lifted her trunk and trumpeted good-bye.

On the plane, Maggie's keepers kept her calm and offered her water, fruits, and vegetables. As a special treat, she got M&Ms® and Skittles® too. Veterinarians traveled with Maggie to make sure she was safe and healthy during the long journey.

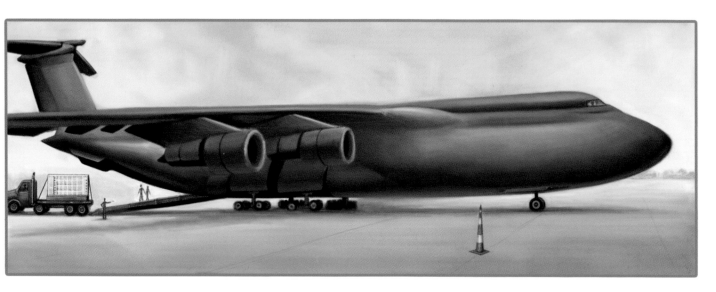

Her human friends were happy for Maggie but worried about her future. Would the group at PAWS accept her? She was 24 and had been without another elephant for 10 years.

When Maggie arrived at PAWS, Michelle was waiting. Maggie stretched out her trunk. She placed it into Michelle's hand to say hello. Michelle blew into her trunk, an elephant kiss. "Hello, Maggie!" exclaimed Michelle. Maggie rumbled back her greeting.

Maggie got out of the crate. The vets checked her. It was too early to release her with the group of four African elephants; but she could see and smell them, and they could see and smell her. Because she had been so sick in Alaska, she needed to regain her strength. The staff encouraged her to walk up and down hills. For the first time, Maggie learned to push over a tree, a favorite sport of wild elephants.

For weeks, Maggie adapted to her surroundings and healed. Then, it was time for her to meet her group.

The staff released Maggie from her stall. She saw the other elephants and loped towards them with her ears out. She threw her trunk in their direction to let them know she was an elephant.

Across a fence, Maggie looked at her group—Mara, Ruby, Lulu, and the matriarch, whose name was 71. They reached through the fence and touched each other. They ate near each other. And, they talked—rumbling noises and infrasonic sounds that humans cannot hear. For a while, Maggie and the group remained near each other, parted only by the fence.

Finally, Maggie was strong enough to be with the group. The staff nervously opened her gate. Maggie might be big but she is little for an African elephant. Maggie lumbered towards the other elephants.

Immediately, four bulky bodies surrounded her, roaring, trumpeting, and rumbling. Maggie looked at her group. Then, she turned and backed into the other elephants.

Just like that, Maggie was home.

At PAWS, Maggie is never alone. Strong and happy, she rarely strays from her best friend, Lulu. Mara often joins them. They walk the hills, eat old tree branches, and graze on grass. They play in water holes and take mud baths, much like they would in the wild.

When Lulu sleeps, Maggie stands over her. The two even share a stall in the elephants' barn. At night, the elephants get treats, like popcorn, stuffed into Boomer® balls.

And the best part?

With elephant friends of her own,
Maggie no longer needs that tire.

For Creative Minds

Elephant Herds

Elephants are very smart, social animals. In the wild, elephants live in herds with their extended family. They bond at an early age and they take care of each other. Usually, related females stay together for life while males often go off on their own, make friends with other families, or join other all-male groups.

The female leader, the mighty matriarch, is in charge. She is usually the oldest elephant and has a very good memory. Her job is to lead her herd to grazing sites, favorite watering holes, shaded areas, and safe places to spend the night. Big elephants have big appetites and pachyderms spend up to 20 hours every day foraging, looking for food. They also like to play, bathe, and rest. Elephants can sleep standing up or lying down. When one elephant lies down, another elephant often stands over her, watching her.

Mothers give birth every four to six years and have one baby at a time. Babies' mothers, sisters, aunts, and cousins all care for the young ones, especially as they struggle to learn how to use that long, funny trunk. Every day, elephants communicate with each other through many different sounds, including those that humans cannot hear, as well as gestures, like stomping and flapping their ears. They act like a family unit. When an elephant dies, the rest of the herd mourns.

Zoos

Today's zookeepers have a deep understanding of wild animals and their natural history. Zookeepers try to give their elephants opportunities to exercise, learn, and be in the company of other elephants, as much as possible. Keepers take notes on what the elephants eat and drink, what medicines they take, and their behaviors to ensure they are happy and healthy.

In zoos, exhibits are as large and natural as possible to accommodate groups of elephants who like to roam around and look for food, as well as places to rest and to play. Exhibits might have steep hills and flat spaces, shady areas, watering holes (or streams), and perhaps a mud hole for wallowing. Since elephants need to walk and forage, food may be scattered around the habitat. Hay may be suspended in nets above the elephants' heads so that they have to reach for it, strengthening their neck, back, and trunk muscles. Elephants need to use their large brains, so keepers give them puzzles to solve. When the keepers place chopped up food in barrels with holes in them, the elephants have to figure out the puzzle to get the food. On hot days, the elephants may have a chance to eat huge frozen popsicles. They play with crush-proof toys, Boomer® balls and milk crates.

In zoos, elephants do not perform tricks. Training is all about staying safe and healthy. For example, sometimes elephants in zoos don't get enough exercise and their feet get sore. A keeper may train an elephant to touch her foot to a bar or foot rest. Teaching an elephant to put her foot in place and hold it there gives the keeper time to carefully and safely check her foot and nails.

Sometimes an animal like Maggie is not thriving in the zoo. When this happens, the keepers try their best to take care of the animal. They might change the animal's diet or provide different activities for the animal. If the animal is sick, the keepers make sure the animal gets medical care. If a zoo cannot meet an animal's needs, they find a new place where the animal can live. They might send the animal to a different zoo or to an animal sanctuary.

If you were an elephant keeper, what would you do:

- to take care of the elephant?
- to help the elephant make friends?
- if the elephant got sick?
- if the elephant seemed sad?
- if the elephant needed a new home?

Q&A with Keeper Michelle Harvey

How much food does Maggie eat?

Maggie eats approximately 250 pounds of food a day, but this can vary by season. Her diet consists of hay, grasses, bark, browse (like oak, acacia, and bamboo) herbivore pellets, bran, bread, and fresh fruits and vegetables. Maggie forages for her own food during the day. In the evening, she eats inside the barn.

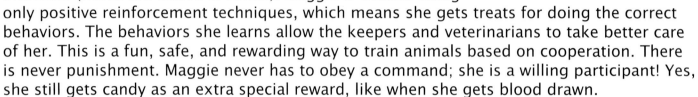

What is Maggie's favorite food? Does she still get candy for obeying commands?

Maggie's favorite foods are bananas, crusty bread, and acacia branches (which are native to Africa). Maggie is trained using only positive reinforcement techniques, which means she gets treats for doing the correct behaviors. The behaviors she learns allow the keepers and veterinarians to take better care of her. This is a fun, safe, and rewarding way to train animals based on cooperation. There is never punishment. Maggie never has to obey a command; she is a willing participant! Yes, she still gets candy as an extra special reward, like when she gets blood drawn.

Are there any foods that she hates?

Maggie dislikes eggplant, lemons, and limes. She will throw them back at you!

How much does Maggie weigh?

Maggie weighs approximately 8,300 pounds, about the size of a pickup truck. She stands on a scale that is placed in a chute and walks across it to exit the barn. She is rewarded with treats for standing still so we can record her weight.

Does she only drink water?

Yes, Maggie only drinks water, and she likes it really warm. An elephant trunk holds 2.5 gallons of water at a time. Maggie can drink up to 80 gallons a day, as much as two bathtubs full of water.

Michelle Harvey and Maggie

Does Maggie do tricks?

Maggie does not do tricks but she is free to express herself as an elephant would. She loves to splatter herself in mud, rub her trunk over the other elephants, pull branches off the trees, and chase a flock of turkeys!

Does she have any toys?

Yes. She has a giant Boomer® ball with holes in it. We fill the ball with treats. She rolls and kicks it so that the treats fall out. Maggie and the other elephants also play with logs and branches. They throw them in the air and carry them on their backs. Maggie also loves water play!

How loud is Maggie?

Maggie is very vocal. She rumbles, roars, and purrs. When she gets excited or greets another elephant, she trumpets as loud as a jet engine!

Was it hard for Maggie to adapt to the warm weather after being in Alaska for so long?

No. Warm weather is the natural environment for an elephant. This is great for Maggie.

What is a day in the life of Maggie like at PAWS?

Maggie spends her days with other elephants. Lulu is her best friend. She also has Mara, Thika, and Toka, all of whom explore grass, trees, mud holes, a seasonal lake, and rolling hills with her. The weather is often sunny and warm. On cold nights, she can sleep in a heated barn but usually prefers to nap on the grass. She receives a warm bath every day and will rumble or trumpet in delight! Caregivers prepare her morning and evening meals (grain, bran, vitamin supplements, fruits, vegetables, and hay) but once outside, she eats grasses, leaves, and bark. We trim and inspect her feet during training sessions. This is when she may get candy as a special treat! Her day is about doing what she wants. She is never forced to do anything or punished in anyway. She has the freedom just to be an elephant.

How can you tell if Maggie is happy?

I really am not sure if Maggie is happy. She is living a life in captivity instead of being in the wild with her family; but it makes me happy to know she isn't alone. She has elephant friends and a peaceful environment at PAWS. She is loved by all of us who take care of her.

Animal Enrichment

Animals need to keep their brain and senses busy! Would you want to sit in one place all the time with nothing to do? No! Neither do animals. Keepers come up with ways to help the animals exercise their body and mind. This is called animal enrichment.

Keepers create a schedule and continually change activities to keep the elephants interested. They place tasty treats, like carrots, bananas, popsicles, or popcorn, in different places, so that the elephant has to stretch to reach them. New smells, like spices, vinegar, cat nip, or chapstick, give the elephants something to discover and think about. Textured objects, like tree branches, mulch, tires, Boomer® balls, and bouncy balls, are fun for the elephants to touch and move around. Elephants can move around between different play spaces, like waterfalls, streams, and shaded areas

How do you exercise your body and your mind? You might say these are your human enrichment activities!

To Pat Lampi, the Executive Director of the Alaska Zoo, whose courage, commitment, and conviction I admire greatly.—JKC

For my mother and father.—PS

Thanks to the following for taking such great care of Maggie and for verifying the accuracy of the information in this book:
· Pat Lampi, Executive Director at the Alaska Zoo
· Michelle Harvey, one of Maggie's keepers
· Performing Animal Welfare Society (PAWS) staff

Maggie's current home is made possible by PAWS founders Ed Stewart and the late Pat Derby, along with all of PAWS' elephant caregivers—a dedicated team led by Brian Busta and veterinarian Dr. Jackie Gai.

Library of Congress Cataloging in Publication Control Number: 2017040945

Cataloging Information is available through the Library of Congress:

9781607184508	English hardcover ISBN
9781607184614	English paperback ISBN
9781607184669	Spanish paperback ISBN
9781607184836	English ebook downloadable ISBN
9781607184881	Spanish ebook downloadable ISBN

Interactive, read-aloud ebook features selectable English (9781607185147) and Spanish (9781607185192) text and audio (web and iPad/tablet based)

Translated into Spanish: *Maggie, el último elefante en Alaska*

Lexile® Level: 620L

key phrases: zoos, elephants, animal rescue, animal sanctuary, transportation

Bibliography:
Hare, Tony. Animal Fact File: Head-to-tail Profiles of over 90 Mammals. Singapore: Facts On File, 1999. 52-53. Print.
Jenkins, Martin, and Ivan Bates. Grandma Elephant's in Charge. Cambridge, MA: Candlewick, 2003. Print.
Moss, Cynthia, and Martyn Colbeck. Little Big Ears: The Story of Ely. New York: Simon & Schuster, 1997. Print.
O'Connell, Caitlin, Donna M. Jackson, and T. C. Rodwell. The Elephant Scientist. Boston: Houghton Mifflin for Children, 2011. Print.
Whittaker, Margaret, and Gail Laule. "Chapter 13: Protected Contact and Elephant Welfare." Endangered Species and Wetland Report. Endangered Species & Wetlands Report/Poplar Publishing, n.d. Web.
"Welcome to ElephantVoices." Welcome to ElephantVoices. ElephantVoices, n.d. Web.
"Performing Animal Welfare Society -- PAWS." Performing Animal Welfare Society -- PAWS. N.p., n.d. Web.
SitNews, and Http://www.sitnews.us. "SitNews: Alaska Elephant Finds New Home With Help of Air Force by Staff Sgt. Francesca Popp." SitNews: Alaska Elephant Finds New Home With Help of Air Force by Staff Sgt. Francesca Popp. Stories In The News. Ketchikan, AK, n.d. Web.

Manufactured in China, December 2017
This product conforms to CPSIA 2008
First Printing

Arbordale Publishing
Mt. Pleasant, SC 29464
www.ArbordalePublishing.com